MW00786271

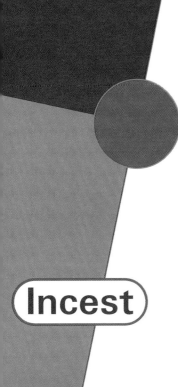

Incest

"Why Am I Afraid to Tell?"

by Kate Havelin

Consultant:
Martha Farrell Erickson, PhD
Director of Children, Youth, and Family Consortium
University of Minnesota

Perspectives on Relationships

LifeMatters
an imprint of Capstone Press
Mankato, Minnesota

LifeMatters books are published by Capstone Press
818 North Willow Street • Mankato, Minnesota 56001
http://www.capstone-press.com

Printed in the United States of America

Library of Congress Cataloging-in-Publication Data
    Havelin, Kate, 1961–
    Incest: why am I afraid to tell? / by Kate Havelin.
         p.   cm. — (Perspectives on relationships)
    Includes bibliographical references and index.
    Summary: Describes incest, its possible causes, its effects, and what can be done to stop it.
    ISBN 0-7368-0288-6 (book). — ISBN 0-7368-0295-9
    1. Incest—United States Juvenile literature. 2. Incest—United States Juvenile literature. [1. Incest. 2. Child sexual abuse.]
    I. Title. II. Series.
    HV6570.7.H38 2000
    364.15´36—dc21   99-31162
                                        CIP

Staff Credits
Rebecca Aldridge, Kristin Thoennes, editors; Adam Lazar, designer; Kimberly Danger, photo researcher

Photo Credits
Cover: Index Stock Photography/©Jenssen
Index Stock Imagery/34
Index Stock Photography, Inc/6, 10, 29
International Stock/©Victor Ramos, 53
Photri, Inc/54, 59; ©Skjold, 26, 47, 50, 58
Photri-Microstock/©Helle Nielsen, 18
PNI/©RubberBall 17
Unicorn Stock Photos/©Deneve Feigh Bunde, 9; ©Tom McCarthy, 14; ©Eric R. Berndt, 25; D & I MacDonald, 33; ©Dennis MacDonald, 36; ©A. Ramey, 39; ©Jeff Greenberg, 44

A 0 9 8 7 6 5 4 3 2 1

This book provided by a
grant from the
Family Resource Council
Merced County
Office of Education

Table of Contents

1	What Are Sexual Abuse and Incest?	4
2	Why Do Adults Sexually Abuse Children?	12
3	How Sexual Abuse Hurts Kids	20
4	How to Break the Silence	30
5	Dealing With Family Once They Know	40
6	Learning to Trust Again	48
7	Important Stuff to Remember	56
	Glossary	60
	For More Information	61
	Useful Addresses and Internet Sites	62
	Index	63

Chapter Overview

Sexual abuse is any sexual activity that is forced on a person. Sexual abuse is against the law.

Sexual abuse includes sexual intercourse, pornography, and exhibitionism.

Incest is sexual abuse between people who are related by birth or marriage.

Many people are afraid to admit that they have been sexually abused.

Many abusers convince their victims to keep sexual abuse a secret.

Chapter 1

What Are Sexual Abuse and Incest?

Mary Beth is scared of her father. He does not hit her.

Mary Beth and Her Father

Instead, he touches her. It started when Mary Beth was seven years old. Her father told her she was daddy's little girl. He made her sit on his lap while he stroked her arms.

Now Mary Beth is 11. She knows it is wrong for her father to touch her breasts. Sometimes he puts his penis in her vagina. Mary Beth closes her eyes because she is afraid. She pretends to be far away. She wishes he would stop. Mary Beth does not know what to do. She loves her father but hates what he does. It makes her feel confused, angry, and afraid.

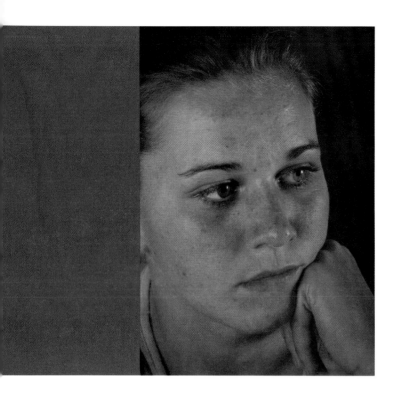

Sexual Abuse

Sexual abuse is any sexual activity that is forced on a person. Usually it involves a young person and someone responsible for that person. The abuser could be a parent, relative, teacher, religious leader, day care provider, bus driver, or baby-sitter. Sexual assault also is any forced sexual activity such as rape. However, when a child is sexually assaulted, the abuser is usually an adult who has no responsibility over that child. For example, a stranger who forced a child to have sex would be guilty of sexual assault. Most state laws treat sexual assault and sexual abuse differently.

Sexual abuse includes behaviors such as:

Fondling, or touching, a child's sex organs—The penis, vagina, breasts, and anus are all considered sex organs.

Intercourse, or penetration of the penis into the vagina

Sodomy, or anal or oral sex—Sodomy includes putting a finger, penis, tongue, or other object in another person's anus or mouth.

Exhibitionism—This occurs when an abuser shows his or her genitals to someone or forces a person to show his or her genitals.

Obscene telephone calls in which the abuser talks about sex

Pornography, or sexual photographs or videotapes intended to sexually excite people who see them

Prostitution, or the selling of sex or other sexual behavior

Incest accounts for half of all sexual abuse cases.

Incest

Most of this book focuses on one specific kind of sexual abuse called incest. Incest is any type of sexual activity between two people who are closely related. Incest offenders can be a victim's parent, brother, sister, aunt, uncle, or cousin. Sometimes stepparents or other people related only by marriage are considered incest offenders.

Some people also consider it incest when someone who seems like a child's guardian sexually abuses that child. For example, a parent's live-in boyfriend or girlfriend may act like a child's guardian. However, that person is not legally related to the child.

Other Kinds of Abuse

Sexual abuse is one of four types of abuse. Often, abused children suffer more than one kind of abuse. The other types of abuse are physical and emotional abuse and neglect.

Physical Abuse

Physical abuse includes any action meant to harm a person's body. Hitting, kicking, slapping, punching, burning, pulling hair, and poisoning are all forms of physical abuse.

Emotional Abuse

Emotional abuse is anything said or done to hurt a person's feelings or sense of self. Unkind words are one kind of emotional abuse. Cruel actions such as locking a child in a dark closet are another type of emotional abuse. Emotional abuse often happens along with other kinds of abuse.

Neglect

Neglect means to ignore or choose not to take care of someone's basic needs. Some parents neglect their child's physical needs for food, clothing, medical care, or shelter. Some may neglect a child's emotional needs for love, kindness, and closeness. Some parents neglect a child's educational needs. Neglect is the most common type of abuse. Look in the back of this book for more information and resources about physical and emotional abuse and neglect.

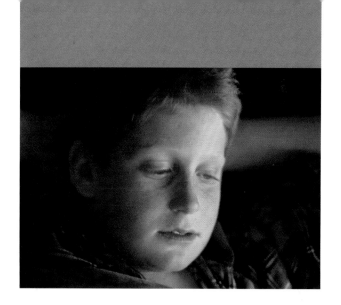

Sexual Abuse Often Is Kept Secret

Many experts think that sexual abuse is the most underreported form of abuse. Children and even adults who find out about sexual abuse often are afraid to report it. Victims may not tell about the abuse for many reasons. They may be afraid no one will believe them. They also may be afraid of what other people will think about them. Victims of incest and other kinds of sexual abuse often feel terrible shame and guilt. However, children and teens who have been sexually abused never are to blame.

Abusers Often Scare Kids Into Silence

Victims of sexual abuse may be afraid of what the abuser will do to them or their family. Abusers often convince their victims to keep the abuse secret. Sometimes abusers threaten to physically hurt or kill their victims if they tell. Some abusers say they will hurt a victim's brother, sister, or other relative.

Many abusers convince their victims to stay silent by using psychological pressure. Abusers may trick their victims into thinking they care about them. Often abusers tell their victims that no one will believe them if they tell. Some incest victims are told they will be kicked out of their home if they report the abuse.

Points to Consider

What is the difference between incest and other kinds of sexual abuse?

Why do you think people do not report being abused?

Why do you think emotional abuse often occurs with other forms of child abuse?

Chapter Overview

No one is sure why sexual abuse happens.

Sexual abusers often share similar traits.

People who have been sexually abused in the past may become abusers themselves.

There is no excuse for sexual abuse.

Sexual abuse can happen to any child or teen, but some children and teens face higher risks for abuse.

Chapter 2

Why Do Adults Sexually Abuse Children?

Berto feels sick. He just found out his friend Carolyn **Berto Listens to His Friend** was sexually abused by her father. Berto cannot believe a father would hurt his own daughter. Carolyn cried when she told Berto what happened.

Berto knows adults can do strange things. But he is shocked to hear Carolyn's story. Berto promised Carolyn that he would not tell anyone, but he is confused. He needs to talk with someone. He goes home and looks on-line to find out more about incest. He wants to help his friend and to try to understand why abuse happens.

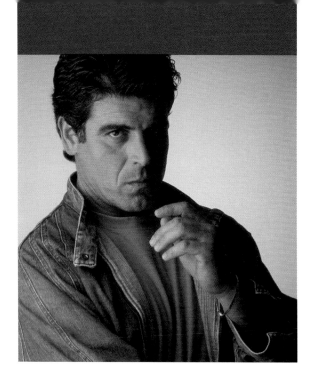

Common Traits of Abusers

Why an adult would sexually abuse a child is hard to understand. It is even tougher to understand how a parent could abuse his or her own child. Little research has been done to explain sexual abuse of children. Experts do not know why this abuse happens. They do know, however, some common traits that many abusers share.

Almost all sexual abusers are men.

Men are responsible for about 89 percent of sexual abuse cases. Women account for about 12 percent of sexual abuse cases.

Abusers usually know their victims.

Some studies show that 99 percent of sexual abuse victims knew their abusers. More than half of the abusers seduced, or tempted, their victims.

More than half of adult sexual abusers say they were 17 years or younger when they first committed abuse.

More Caucasian parents abuse their children than do parents of other races.

Caucasian, or white, children and teens are more likely to be sexually abused by their birth parents than by other people. Children of other races are more likely to be sexually abused by people other than their birth parents. About 70 percent of sex offenders, or people who have committed sexual crimes, are white.

Poverty increases the risk of sexual abuse.

Children from families with an income of less than $15,000 a year are 18 times more likely to be sexually abused than other kids are.

Sexual abusers often are married.

More than half—64 percent—of sex offenders are either married or divorced. Most abusers have heterosexual attractions. That means they are attracted to people of the opposite sex.

Children ages eight and older are more likely to be physically, sexually, or emotionally abused than younger kids are. Younger children are more likely to be neglected, especially medically neglected, than are older kids.

Sexual abusers have normal intelligence.
Eighty percent of all sexual abusers have normal intelligence. Most abusers are not mentally ill.

Many sexual abusers start at a young age.
Some experts believe that teenage boys commit half of all sexual abuse. Researchers believe that many of those young offenders were abused themselves. More than 20 percent of sexual abusers say they were abused as children. Violence is a learned behavior. Children see the way their parents and other adults act. When children get older, they may imitate what they have seen. Being a victim of abuse does not make it okay to abuse others. However, it may explain why some sexual abuse happens.

Risk Factors for Abuse
Any child or teen can be abused. Children and teens need to know they are not responsible for being sexually abused. They are not to blame. Parents and other adults hurt children for their own reasons. Incest never happens because a child or teen did something wrong.

Sexual abuse happens to all kinds of kids, but some children face greater risks of being abused. Risk factors for sexual abuse include age, gender, and race.

Age

Even babies can be sexually abused. However, most sexual abuse happens to children age three or older. Most sexual abuse begins before children reach puberty. That means the abuse starts before a child's body develops pubic hair and mature sex organs.

The percentage of children who are sexually abused rises as children get older. Teens suffer the highest rates of sexual abuse. Children ages 12 and older account for 35 percent of sexual abuse victims. Some teens may be better able to defend themselves against abuse than younger children. Unfortunately, many teens run away from home to avoid sexual abuse. Homeless teens, however, often end up experiencing even more abuse.

Gender

Girls are three times more likely to be sexually abused than boys are. Also, girls are more likely to be victims of incest. Boys, on the other hand, are more likely to be victims of abusers from outside their family.

Men are most likely to abuse girls. Both men and women abuse boys. Most men who abuse boys consider themselves to be heterosexual. Sexual abuse has less to do with sexual attraction and more to do with power and control.

Race

Caucasian children are more likely to be sexually abused than children of other races are. African-American children are much less likely to be sexually abused than are Caucasian children. African-American children face a higher rate of other kinds of abuse. Researchers do not know why risk differs among races. Differences in cultural beliefs and taboos, or things that are forbidden, may influence risk.

Up to 30 percent of women and about 10 percent of men had sexual contact with a much older person while they were growing up.

Did You Know?

Points to Consider

Many people think abusers stand out or look different from other people. Do you think that is true? Explain.

Why do you think sexual abusers usually hurt someone they know rather than a stranger?

Why do you think adults sexually abuse children? In what ways do you think children have less power than adults do?

Why do you think some sexual abuse victims become abusers themselves?

Chapter Overview

Children and teens who are sexually abused experience a variety of emotions.

Abuse affects boys and girls in ways that are both similar and different.

Sexual abuse can cause long-term physical or psychological problems for victims.

Abused children and teens need to get medical help after being abused.

Chapter 3

How Sexual Abuse Hurts Kids

Steve's neighbor sexually abuses him.
The physical experience feels good,
Steve Is Confused
but it also makes Steve feel confused and ashamed. He knows
no adult should play with a boy's penis. Steve cannot
understand how something wrong can seem so natural.

Steve learned about "good touch, bad touch" in school. He
thought if someone abused him, it would hurt and feel like a
bad touch. But Steve's body enjoys the neighbor's touch. Still,
Steve wishes his neighbor would leave him alone.
Unfortunately, Steve does not know how to stop it. He thinks
no one will believe him. He is afraid people will blame him.
Steve wishes it were all just a bad dream.

How Abuse Makes Children Feel

One of the worst results of sexual abuse is how it makes children and teens feel about themselves. They may feel ashamed, guilty, confused, mistrustful, angry, helpless, afraid, isolated, or suicidal.

Shame

Children who have been abused often feel dirty. They may feel like no one else will ever love or respect them. They may feel humiliated, or embarrassed. Some children and teens worry they will disgrace their family if they say they have been sexually abused.

Guilt

All sexual abuse is wrong. It is always the abuser, never the victim, who has done something bad. However, children and teens who have been abused often feel guilty. They may feel they led the abuser on. Nothing a child or teen says, does, or wears leads to abuse. Victims never are guilty.

Incest

Confusion

Sexual abuse confuses many victims. It does not always hurt physically. Sometimes what a sexual abuser does makes the victim's body feel good. That is natural. The human body is made to respond pleasurably to sexual stimulation. Even if the experience felt good, the abuser's behavior is still abuse. Some people who have been sexually abused may not feel like victims. They may love or care for their abuser. However, it is important to know the abuser has done something wrong.

Mistrust

Many children believe adults will help them. Their parents teach them right from wrong and protect them. Children who are sexually abused learn a different message. They learn that adults can hurt them. That message is especially true for children who experience incest. Instead of protecting them from others, their own parents abuse them.

Not surprisingly, sexually abused children and teens find it hard to trust people. At least one adult has betrayed them. They become wary or suspicious of letting anyone get close to them. Abused children often do not even trust themselves. They may believe they are responsible for what happened. They may think they should have said or done something to stop the abuser. They may resent the way their body reacted to the abuse.

Anger

People who have been sexually abused often are angry. They are mad that their body has been abused and that their peace of mind has been stolen.

Helplessness

Victims of sexual abuse may feel that they have lost control of their body as well as their life. They may feel helpless to stop their abuser. Those feelings make it hard for victims to feel good about themselves and begin healing.

Fear

Children and teens who have been abused often fear it will happen again. Many times, they have good reason for that fear. Many abusers continue to abuse their victim for months or even years. Victims also may fear for their brothers or sisters. For example, a father who abuses one daughter also may abuse other family members.

The fear that children live with affects them. It may make them timid or depressed. It may make them overly aggressive. Either way, it is very hard for a person to live with fear.

Isolation

Abused children and teens often feel isolated, or alone. They do not want anyone to know their secret. They may feel they have nothing in common with other kids. Often, abused children avoid getting close to others, even though they may feel lonely.

Suicide

Sometimes victims of sexual abuse think about suicide. They may feel hopeless about their situation. However, suicide never is a solution. Suicidal feelings are a signal the person needs to get help from someone he or she trusts.

The Different Effects on Boys and Girls

Many people mistakenly assume only females are sexually abused. Also, our society sends messages to boys that they should be tough and able to defend themselves. That makes it difficult for boys to admit that they have been abused. Both boys and girls deserve protection from abuse.

Boys and girls usually react differently to abuse. Girls are likely to become depressed. Boys often become more aggressive and are more likely to end up sexually abusing others. Boys may believe they need to act tough to prove themselves. They may be trying to protect themselves from being hurt again.

Boys who are sexually abused by women may worry if they did not enjoy the experience. Sometimes messages from our society may lead boys to believe that they should always want sex. However, sexual abuse is much different from having sex. Boys who are abused by men may worry that people will think they are gay, or attracted to other males.

Mei Tries to Cope

Mei cannot escape from her stepfather's abuse. She cannot get away from him, so she tries to run away mentally. When he touches her, her mind blocks him out. She pretends to be a different person. After years of blocking out the pain, Mei's mind is troubled. Part of her is used to the abuse and seems wild. It scares the part of Mei that tries to ignore the abuse.

Sometimes Mei feels overwhelmed. She does not know who she is anymore. Her teachers send her to the school counselor. It helps to talk to someone. The counselor listens to Mei. She refers Mei to a psychologist, a doctor who helps people with emotional problems. This psychologist specializes in helping abused children.

Abuse Can Cause Physical and Psychological Problems

Abused children sometimes have serious physical and psychological problems as a result of the abuse. They include sexually transmitted diseases, unwanted pregnancy, and post-traumatic stress and other personality disorders.

Sexually Transmitted Diseases

Sexual abuse can make a person physically sick. Some diseases are transmitted through sexual contact. Abusers who have sexually transmitted diseases (STDs) can pass those diseases on to their victims. Herpes, gonorrhea, and HIV and AIDS are some examples of STDs.

It is important that abused children and teens be tested to make sure they were not infected. Often people have no symptoms of these diseases. Symptoms can take months or years to appear. Doctors can help people who have been infected. It is essential to get treatment quickly after infection. Not all STDs are curable, but they are all treatable. The sooner they are discovered, the less damage they can do to a person's body.

The following hotlines can give incest victims more information or referrals regarding STDs, pregnancy, or sexual abuse.

STD Hotlines
National AIDS Hotline 1-800-342-AIDS
Sexually Transmitted Disease Hotline 1-800-227-8922

Pregnancy Hotline
Planned Parenthood Hotline 1-800-230-7526

Sexual Abuse Hotlines
Rape, Abuse & Incest National Network 1-800-656-HOPE
National Child Abuse Hotline 1-800-422-4453

Pregnancy

Any girl who has reached puberty can become pregnant. A doctor can do a quick pregnancy test. Any girl who has been sexually abused should be tested. Many cities have women's health clinics that specialize in reproductive health care. That means they help people in regard to having children. These clinics can be found in the phone book under *Pregnancy Counseling.*

Post-Traumatic Stress or Other Personality Disorders

Sexual abuse also can cause victims to have psychological problems. Children who are abused may try to block out the abuse. They may pretend they are somewhere else while the abuse is happening. They may deny the abuse actually happened.

Some sexual abuse victims have post-traumatic stress disorder (PTSD). It also is called post-traumatic stress syndrome. This disorder can happen to people who have any kind of emotional shock. Burn victims and soldiers who have fought in war also may have PTSD.

Some experts believe abuse victims often have chronic trauma disorder. That is a combination of PTSD and other psychological problems. Abuse also triggers the other problems. Children who are abused often grow up with a distorted view of themselves and the world. That means their view has been twisted. They may need help to sort out the many issues they face.

Ignoring pain causes more problems later. People who have been sexually abused are more likely than other people to abuse alcohol or other drugs. Also, abused children and teens who do not get help often face sexuality problems later in life.

Points to Consider

Do you think our society sends different messages about sex to boys and girls? Explain.

How would you help a friend who said she or he was being abused?

Look in the phone book and find the numbers of three places that could help incest victims.

Chapter Overview

Sexual abuse does not stop by itself. Someone needs to intervene, or do something.

Many people can help children and teens who have been sexually abused.

Teachers, doctors, and many other professionals must report any suspected child abuse.

Abused children and teens often must tell their stories to many people before their case is settled.

Chapter 4

How to Break the Silence

People who are being sexually abused can do something to stop
the abuse. Breaking the cycle of abuse is not easy. It takes
courage. However, victims of abuse do have power over the
abuser to break the silence.

Many cases of child abuse involve older children abusing younger children. Some estimates show that teen boys are responsible for half of all sexual abuse of children.

Betsy Shares Her Secret

Betsy dreads going to bed. Betsy's older brother Jim comes into her room every night. He forces Betsy to have sex with him.

Betsy is afraid to tell because Jim has threatened her. She hates Jim, and she hates herself. Sometimes she thinks she wants to kill herself. She knows she cannot keep living this way.

One night after Jim has been unusually rough, Betsy decides she must tell someone. However, she does not know whom to tell. She is exhausted and scared. The next day she decides to go to the school nurse. Betsy does not want to keep her secret anymore.

The school nurse listens and tells Betsy she believes her. She says that Betsy must tell her parents. The nurse calls Betsy's parents. They listen to Betsy and are shocked. The school nurse and counselor talk with Betsy and her parents. They tell them that Jim and Betsy both need help.

Incest

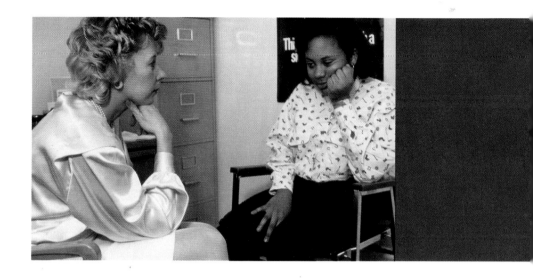

Telling Someone

Telling someone about sexual abuse is hard, but it is important to make the effort. Keeping abuse a secret hurts victims. A friend may tell you he or she is being abused and ask you to keep the secret. You will help your friend more by telling a trusted adult. Telling this kind of secret is okay.

You may tell someone who does not believe you. Do not let that stop you. Incest seldom stops by itself. Abusers usually cannot stop abusing without help. Keep telling people about the abuse until someone listens and helps. People will help you. Do not be afraid or embarrassed to report abuse.

Many people know what incest is like. Many adults who have survived incest work to help others, especially children and teens. Many groups of incest survivors also exist to help.

Ways to Get Help

Chances are you already know someone who can help. Maybe you could talk with a trusted adult such as a neighbor, teacher, or coach.

Professionals also can help you. Teachers, doctors, nurses, police, and social workers must report child abuse. The law requires professionals to report any suspected cases of child abuse to police or child protection services.

There also are organizations that work to help victims of abuse. The chart on the next page lists some numbers you can call for help. You also can look in a phone book under *Child Welfare, Child Protection Services,* or *Social Services.* The back of this book lists other options.

One estimate showed that only **10 percent** of sexual abuse cases are reported to police or social services.

Hotlines

These hotlines are answered 24 hours a day. Numbers that begin with 1-800 do not cost any money, even from a pay phone. Staff members who answer hotlines can refer you to someone in your area who can help.

Boys Town 1-800-448-3000
For either boys or girls in the United States and Canada

Childhelp USA,
The National Child Abuse Hotline 1-800-422-4453

Covenant House Nineline 1-800-999-999
Geared to runaways or kids who are thinking of running away

Kids Help Phone 1-800-668-6868
For Canadian children and teens

What Happens When You Tell

Sexual abuse is against the law in every state and province. That means police or other authorities need to investigate all reports of abuse. Often child protection workers handle cases of sexual abuse. These people are trained to talk with and help abused children and teens.

Sexually abused children often have to tell several people about the abuse. They may have to talk with social workers, doctors, police, lawyers, and judges. These people all want to help. Repeating a story of abuse can be painful. The average sexual abuse victim recounts his or her story to eight or more people.

Often victims of sexual abuse also must have a thorough medical exam. A doctor checks the victim's body for signs of abuse. The doctor and medical staff may ask detailed questions about what happened. The interviews, exams, and personal questions may be upsetting. However, the doctors, social workers, and other authorities are all trying to help. They need to know exactly what happened before they can work to stop the abuse.

Here is a brief summary of what can happen once incest is reported.

The victim may stay with his or her family while social workers investigate the case. Sometimes, child protection workers ask families to get counseling or other services.

A judge can order that the victim and the abuser be separated. Sometimes that means a judge orders the suspected abuser to leave the home. Some cities have child visitation centers where children can safely see abusive parents under supervision.

One family may have three or more caseworkers handling their case before it is resolved.

A judge may decide it is safer for the victim to live away from home. He or she may place the victim in a foster home while the case is investigated. Foster homes are places where children can live safely, away from abusive parents or relatives. Judges want to make sure children and teens are safe. They are not punishing kids by sending them to foster homes. Instead, courts are trying to protect children and teens who are at risk.

Police may arrest a suspected abuser. The abuser may be held in jail only briefly. Judges who believe children are at risk sometimes can keep abusers in jail longer.

Officials may charge the abuser with crimes. Then the case can be heard in court. The crimes may be either criminal or civil. People who are found guilty of criminal crimes may be fined or sent to prison. People found guilty of civil crimes may pay fines or be required to get help.

"Each time you reach out for help, you defeat your abusers. You have not let them destroy you."
—Ellen Bass, *Beginning to Heal*

Terri Goes to Court

It has been a year since Terri told her grandmother that she was being abused. She kept her dad's abuse secret for three years. Now many people know about the incest.

Terri hates being interviewed by police and lawyers. Terri's caseworker told Terri that officials need to understand what has happened to her. Terri tries to be patient. She answers the same questions again and again.

Terri knows she must answer those painful questions in court tomorrow. Sometimes she feels like giving up, but she thinks of her little sister, Pam. Terri knows that telling her story is the best way to protect Pam. She wants Pam to be safe.

Going to Court Takes Time

Unfortunately, justice is not quick. Some families wait months or even years for their case to be heard. During that time, it is hard for incest victims to get on with their life. Criminal cases often take longer to get to court than civil court cases. The average family court case takes one year. Families often must appear in court at least once a month while their case is active.

Reporting incest is a serious decision. It is important that victims keep a record of the abuse. Writing in a diary or telling a friend is a good idea. It helps to keep anything that may prove the abuse happened.

Points to Consider

Who would you tell if you were sexually abused?

Why do you think a judge would remove a child or teen from his or her home?

Why do you think it is important to keep a record of abuse?

Chapter Overview

Reporting incest takes great courage.

Incest can divide families.

Children and teens whose family does not support them can still find others who will believe them.

Abused children need to take care of themselves if their parents will not protect them.

Reports of incest often can lead to parents' divorce.

Chapter 5

Dealing With Family Once They Know

Breaking the Silence Takes Courage

Incest can devastate children and teens. Unfortunately, telling about incest can be devastating as well. Sometimes children who report incest end up being hurt even more. Some people may not believe them. Their abuser may deny everything and be trusted.

Claire's Family Reacts

Claire's mother was stunned to learn that her husband has abused her daughter. Claire was afraid her mother would hate her. Instead, Claire's mother hugged her. They cried together, and then Claire's mom called the police.

Claire's stepfather denies everything. He swears Claire made up everything. Everyone in the family has had several interviews with lawyers and police. Lawyers and caseworkers are still working on Claire's case. Her stepfather moved out and will go on trial in a few months.

The family is already split up. Claire's mom filed for divorce. Claire's stepsisters blame Claire. Their grandparents and some family friends are divided. Some believe Claire. Others think Claire's stepfather is innocent. Claire feels like she broke up her family. But she knows she told the truth. Claire's psychologist reminds her that she did nothing wrong. It was her stepfather who did something wrong. His crimes have hurt their family.

Reporting incest can break a family apart. However, splitting one's family may be better than secretly suffering. No one deserves to be abused. Victims of incest have the right to report the abuse and to get help. It may take dividing the family or even going to court to stop abuse. However, victims deserve to live peacefully without abuse.

Telling can make the victim feel better. It is a way for victims to take control of the situation and their life. Breaking the silence about abuse can help victims. It also may protect others. Brothers or sisters, friends, and other children may be saved from abuse if victims step forward. Once the abuse is reported, the abuser may begin to get the help he or she needs.

Helping Yourself

Unfortunately, some families do not stand up for their children. Some children and teens who break the silence about incest are treated badly. You may be a victim of incest. If so, here are some suggestions that can help you deal with family once everyone knows about the abuse.

Seek out supportive relatives.

Maybe some family members believe you while others believe your abuser. You need to find relatives who will support you. They may be grandparents, older siblings who have moved out, aunts, uncles, or cousins. Seek out those people who are sympathetic. They can help you through this hard time.

Do what you need to do for yourself.

You need to think about yourself. Doing whatever it takes to stop the abuse is not selfish. You deserve to be safe. A child or teen whose family does not believe him or her must find others for support. Find a friend, therapist, or spiritual leader who will listen to you and offer guidance. A therapist is trained in physical, mental, and behavioral disorders. You also can call an incest hotline. You deserve to find people who can help you.

Be kind to yourself.

Children who have been sexually abused have gone through a terrible trauma, or emotional shock. For some people, drugs and alcohol may seem to numb the pain. However, these substances cannot solve a problem. Instead, drugs and alcohol can create new problems. It is better to deal with your pain now. Otherwise, you may spend years of your adult life dealing with it.

Sexually abused children are most likely to suffer serious injuries when their birth parents are the abuser.

Look to the future.

Your life may seem hard now, but it can get better. Eventually, you will move away from your family or abuser. You can work through the pain of abuse and have a healthier life.

Be prepared.

Do what you can to be good to yourself, but also prepare yourself for setbacks. You may not have good relations with your family now or for years. Your abuser may not get the punishment you think he or she deserves. You cannot control what happens to other people. You can try to improve only your own life.

When Abuse Leads to Divorce

Many parents file for divorce when they learn a spouse has sexually abused a child. Divorce can create more stress for a family already dealing with incest. The sexual abuse may be a key factor in divorce. Some lawyers mistrust reports of child abuse that arise during divorce or custody battles. Custody is the legal right to take care of a child. However, research shows that children seldom lie about abuse, even when their parents are divorcing or fighting over custody.

Adults who ignore signs that a child or teen is being sexually abused also are to blame for the abuse.

Chris Finds Support

Chris told his parents that his grandfather abused him. His mom and dad act as if Chris is to blame. Chris knows that telling was the right thing to do. Although his life has become hard in a new way, he still feels better. Chris learned that his grandfather also abused his cousin Tom. The two boys wonder how many other family members also may have been abused. Both boys are going to testify against their grandfather in court. At least now Chris knows his grandfather will not touch anyone else.

Chris is hurt that his parents will not back him up. Luckily, he has found other relatives who support him. His Aunt Louise told him a neighbor attacked her when she was a teenager. Chris knows she understands the pain of sexual abuse. The minister at Chris's church told Chris about a support group for incest survivors. Now Chris does not feel so alone. He has found people who trust him.

Points to Consider

How do you think your family would react if you told them you had been abused?

How would you help a relative who told you he or she had been abused?

Why do you think reports of incest lead to divorce?

Why do you think adults do not always believe a child who says he or she is being sexually abused?

Chapter Overview

Incest victims often have trouble trusting other people. Sexual abuse victims also may mistrust themselves.

Sometimes the mind buries painful memories for self-protection.

Victims must learn to deal with the pain of their abuse before they can heal.

Victims of incest can recover.

Chapter 6

Learning to Trust Again

"Hey, Anisha, want to come with us after school and get a soda?"

Why Anisha Is Alone

"Uh, no thanks. I've got to get home."

Anisha seldom gets together with the other kids in her class. Sometimes they invite her to go along with them, but she usually says no. She does not want to be friends with them. She does not want them to find out she is abused. Anisha worries that kids would be disgusted if they knew her father sexually abused her.

Anisha thinks her mother knows about the abuse, but they have never talked about it. Anisha does not trust either of her parents. Trusting other people also is hard.

Sexual Abuse Victims Mistrust Others

Children who have been sexually abused have been robbed. Their childhood has been stolen. They have lost their sense of safety. The people who were supposed to protect them—their parents—abused them instead. As a result, abused children and teens have trouble trusting people. They are afraid to become close to others.

Being abused makes it hard to have faith in others. Victims of incest may feel even more betrayed if people do not trust them. They may not understand why people such as their family or the police do not believe them. It helps to understand why some people doubt abuse victims.

Memory

Victims who tell about their abuse deserve to be believed. Once in awhile, however, people who were not abused claim that they were. A few people make up stories. Research shows, however, that children seldom lie about being sexually abused. Sometimes what does happen is that a person's memory tricks him or her. A person's memory is not perfect.

Sometimes people remember things that never really happened to them. Experts say young children are more likely than older children to have these kinds of suggested memories. Some adults undergo hypnosis. That means a therapist puts the person in a trance. This is a conscious state in which the person concentrates deeply on something. Some of these people suddenly remember being abused. Those memories may or may not be true.

It is possible to be abused and not remember what happened. Some people who experience great pain try to block it out. They bury their memories of being abused. Some experts think children handle trauma differently from adults. Young minds may block out memories that are too painful to handle. Later, when the child grows up and can handle the pain, the mind remembers.

Psychologists think most people who have been sexually abused remember the abuse. Victims must remember and deal with the pain of that abuse to recover. Before victims can heal, they need to learn to trust themselves.

Fast Fact

Many children are repeatedly abused over months or years. But a child who has been sexually attacked one time can suffer long-term damage. The number of times one is abused is less important than the fact that one has been abused.

Victims May Not Trust Themselves

Perhaps the worst part of incest is how victims lose their sense of self. Often children and teens who have been sexually abused do not trust themselves. They blame themselves for what happened. They may feel their body betrayed them when it simply responded naturally to sexual touch. Victims also may feel their mind betrayed them. They may be confused about their feelings toward the abuser. They may doubt whether what happened to them was really abuse.

Steps to Recovery

Victims of incest can heal. They can learn to trust themselves and others. Recovering from sexual abuse is not easy, but it can be done. The first step toward healing is to admit that the abuse occurred. The pain of incest will not magically disappear. Pretending abuse did not happen will not help victims get better. People often deny painful memories. Sooner or later, victims of sexual abuse must face what happened.

Recovery Does Not Happen Alone

Victims can get help. They can learn to trust their own instincts. They can go from feeling like a victim to feeling like a survivor and even a victor. However, recovery does not happen alone. Children and teens who have been abused need to be able to talk about the incest with at least one person. A therapist can help. Talking with others who have been sexually abused also can help. Support groups offer victims a safe place to talk about their pain.

Lucy is 22. She has her own tiny apartment. She does not have much

Lucy Looks Ahead

furniture, but she loves being at home. She feels safe and normal. Incest ruined Lucy's chance for a happy childhood, but Lucy is determined to enjoy the rest of her life.

She is doing the hard work of recovering. She meets with her therapist every Wednesday. Once a month, she goes to a support group. Lucy has become friends with two of the women in her group. It helps to talk with people who understand what incest is like.

Sometimes Lucy still feels bad about being abused. Sometimes she cries. Sometimes she gets angry. Lucy knows she cannot change the past. However, she can have more control over the rest of her life. Lucy works to make her life happy and healthy. She does not try to block out the pain. Through therapy she has learned that she must deal with the pain before she can heal.

Anger Can Help You

Once a person begins talking about the abuse, he or she may feel extremely angry. Anger is natural, but it can be scary. Sometimes people say and do things in anger that they might regret. Anger also can make people bitter. However, anger also can help people. The list below includes some healthy ways to express anger.

Write letters to the abuser. (The letters don't need to be mailed.)

Talk with others about incest.

Take a self-defense class.

Destroy something from the abuser.

Scream into a pillow.

Beat up a stuffed animal.

"The most important thing to remember is that you are not alone."
—Kimberlee Ratliff, sexual abuse survivor

If you have been abused, it is okay to be angry with your abuser. You do not have to forgive him or her. You only have to forgive yourself. It is important not to blame yourself for what happened. The sooner you can forgive yourself, the sooner you can heal. As you recover, you can learn to trust other people. You can let yourself grow close to people with whom you feel safe.

Points to Consider

Why do you think incest destroys trust?

Do you think incest victims have a harder time learning to trust than other types of sexual abuse victims do? Why or why not?

Can you think of healthy ways to use anger instead of hurting yourself or others?

Why do you think it is so important for abuse victims to forgive themselves?

Chapter Overview

Incest never is the victim's fault.

Children and teens should not keep incest a secret.

All victims of sexual abuse deserve to be loved, respected, and protected.

Victims of incest are not alone.

Chapter 7

Important Stuff to Remember

Incest is a horrible crime. No child or teen deserves to be sexually abused. No adult should ever have sex with a child.
Unfortunately, some adults do terrible things to kids. Children and teens need to do what they can to help themselves. Here are some key points to keep in mind:

1. Incest never is the victim's fault.
Incest victims often feel shame and guilt. They are not to blame. The abuser is guilty. Children and teens who have been sexually abused are innocent. They never are responsible for the abuse.

2. Children and teens should not keep incest a secret.
Abusers often threaten or force their victims to remain silent.
Secrecy protects the abuser, and it hurts victims. Victims need to
tell someone they trust that they have been hurt. Only then can
things begin to get better. Only then can victims get the help and
protection they deserve.

**3. All victims of sexual abuse deserve to be loved, respected,
and protected.**
It does not matter what a person was forced to do. The person still
deserves to be loved and has the right to be respected. The person
still needs protection and owes it to himself or herself to get help.
Many groups and professionals are trained to aid victims of
incest.

4. Victims of incest are not alone.

Sexual abuse can make a child or teen feel terribly isolated.
Victims of sexual abuse need to remember that they are not alone.
Thousands of children are sexually abused each year. Victims can
find people who understand what happened to them. Experts
agree that group therapy often helps sexual abuse victims. It helps
them see that others have experienced and survived similar pain.
Incest victims can meet other children and teens who are working
to heal their pain. Victims can recover from the abuse they
suffered, too.

Points to Consider

Who is responsible for sexual abuse?

Why is it so important for victims not to keep incest a
secret?

Why is getting help from professionals important?

What could you do to help someone you know who has
been sexually abused?

Glossary

abuse (uh-BYOOZ)—to treat a person or creature meanly

anus (AY-nuss)—the opening in a person's body where feces, or solid waste, comes out

crime (KRIME)—any action that is against the law

emotional (i-MOH-shuh-nuhl)—relating to feelings

exhibitionism (ek-suh-BI-shuh-ni-zum)—the act of showing the genitals to someone

foster home (FOSS-tur HOHM)—a place where a child can live safely, away from his or her parents

guilt (GILT)—a feeling of shame about doing something wrong

incest (in-SEST)—sexual relations between two people who are related by birth or marriage

neglect (ni-GLEKT)—to ignore or choose not to take care of someone's basic needs

penis (PEE-nus)—a male sex organ

physical (FIZ-uh-kuhl)—relating to the body

pornography (por-NAG-ruh-fee)—any kind of media such as photos, books, movies, or videos designed to arouse sexual feelings

sexual (SEK-shoo-wuhl)—relating to sex

shame (SHAME)—a feeling of guilt or sadness

vagina (vuh-JYE-nuh)—a female sex organ

For More Information

Greenberg, Keith. *Family Abuse: Why Do People Hurt Each Other?* New York: Twenty-First Century Books, 1995.

Havelin, Kate. *Child Abuse: "Why Do My Parents Hit Me?"* Mankato, MN: Capstone Press, 2000.

Hyde, Margaret O. *Know About Abuse.* New York: Walker & Co., 1992.

Hyde, Margaret O., and Elizabeth Forsyth. *The Sexual Abuse of Children and Adolescents: From Infants to Adolescents.* Brookfield, CT: Millbrook, 1997.

Useful Addresses and Internet Sites

National Clearinghouse on Family Violence
Family Violence Prevention Division
Health Promotion and Programs Branch
Health Canada
Address Locator 1907D1
Jeanne Mance Building
Tunney's Pasture
Ottawa, ON K1A 1B4
CANADA
1-800-267-1291 (Canada only)

National Exchange Club Foundation for the
Prevention of Child Abuse
3050 Central Avenue
Toledo, OH 43606-1700

National Network for Youth
1319 F Street Northwest
Suite 401
Washington, DC 20004

The Rape, Abuse and Incest National Network
635-B Pennsylvania Avenue Southeast
Washington, DC 20003
1-800-656-HOPE
http://www.rainn.org

Anonymous Sexual Abuse Recovery
http://www.worldchat.com/public/asarc/
welcome.htm
Offers free on-line self-help support to
Canadian victims and survivors of sexual
abuse

National Organization for Victim Assistance
http://www.try-nova.org
Promotes rights and services for both child and
adult victims of crime and crisis

Prevent Child Abuse America
http://www.childabuse.org
Provides tips for preventing child abuse as
well as facts and statistics

VOICES in Action
http://www.voices-action.org
Provides assistance to victims of incest and
child sexual abuse in becoming survivors and
generates public awareness of incest

Index

abuse, types of, 8–9
abusers, 6, 10–11
    childhood of, 16
    traits of, 14–16
adults, trusted, 33, 34
age, 17
alcohol, 29, 44

blame, 10, 16, 21, 46, 52, 58
blocking out pain, 5, 26, 28, 51, 52, 53

chronic trauma disorder, 29
counselors, 26, 28, 32, 36
court system, 38, 39, 46
custody, 45

divorce, 45
doctors, 27, 28, 34, 36
drugs, 29, 44

emotional abuse, 9
exhibitionism, 7

family, 41–46
feeling
    afraid, 5, 10, 22, 32
    angry, 5, 24, 53, 54–55
    ashamed, 10, 21, 22, 58
    confused, 5, 13, 21, 22, 23, 52
    depressed, 24, 25
    fearful, 22, 24
    guilty, 10, 22, 58
    helpless, 22, 24

    isolated, 22, 25, 59
    mistrustful, 22, 23, 49, 50, 52, 55
    overwhelmed, 26
    suicidal, 22, 25, 32
fondling, 5, 7
foster homes, 37
friends, 13, 33, 39, 43, 44

gay, 26
gender, 17, 18, 24, 25–26
group therapy, 59

heterosexual, 15, 18
homeless, 17
hotlines, 28, 35

incest, 8. *See also* sexual abuse
incest survivors, 46, 52

judges, 36–37

lawyers, 38, 42, 45
love, 58

medical exams, 36
memory, 50–51

neglect, 9, 16
neighbors, 21, 34, 46

obscene telephone calls, 7
officials, 37, 38
organizations, 34. *See also* hotlines

Index continued

parents, 32, 46, 50
personality disorders, 27
physical abuse, 8
physical problems, 27–28
police, 34, 35, 37, 38, 42
pornography, 7
post-traumatic stress disorder
        (PTSD), 27, 28–29
poverty, 15
pregnancy, 27, 28
professionals, 34, 58
prostitution, 7
protection, 25, 58
Protection of Children Against
        Sexual Exploitation, The, 7
psychological pressure, 11
psychological problems, 26, 28–29
psychologists, 26, 42, 51

race, 15, 17, 18
rape, 6
record of abuse, 39
recovery, 52, 53, 55
respect, 58
running away, 17, 27, 35

sex organs, 7
sexual abuse,
        breaking the cycle, 31–39
        definition of, 6–7, 8
        getting help, 34–39
        how it hurts kids, 21–29
        as a learned behavior, 16
        reporting, 10, 33–39, 41, 43
        risk factors for, 16–18
        secret, keeping a, 10, 33, 38, 43,
            58
sexual assault, 6
sexual intercourse, 5, 7
sexually transmitted diseases (STDs),
        27, 28
social workers, 34, 36
sodomy, 7
strangers, 6
stress, 45
support groups, 46, 52, 53
supportive relatives, 44, 46

talking, 13, 33, 36, 38, 43, 58
teachers, 34
therapists, 44, 51, 52, 53. See also
        group therapy
threats, 10, 32